Ben Jacks

The Architect's Tour

Notes for the Design Traveler

Culicidae Architectural Press

an imprint of Culicidae Press, LLC
918 5th Street
Ames, IA 50010
USA
www.culicidaepress.com

editor@culicidaepress.com

Culicidae
Architectural Press

ISBN-10:   1941892027

ISBN-13:   978-1-941892-02-2

Cover photo by Ben Jacks
Cover design and interior layout © 2015 by polytekton.com

For Peggy, Callie, and Hugh

Table of Contents

Acknowledgements

I thank Wild Hawthorn Press and the Estate of Ian Hamilton Finlay for permission to publish my photographs of Little Sparta. I thank Murali Paranandi for inviting me to speak at Miami University and thereby instigating a first consideration of the question of how to be a design tourist. I also thank Mary Rogero, John Weigand, Mary Ben Bonham, and Gülen Çevik, who furthered that initial essay with their enthusiastic support. Former students Meili Price and John Welsh deserve my gratitude for providing honest and valuable criticism of an early draft. The Miami University Dolibois European Center staff, Raymond Manes, Crici Dumont, Fannie Blaise, and Laurent Peters, all graciously supported my student study tours. I thank Shannon Van Kirk for her inspiration and a librarian's invaluable professional perspective. Peggy Shaffer set in motion the year abroad with our children Callie and Hugh, and enthusiastically made hundreds of journeys and pilgrimages; I owe her more than I can say.

Preface

In 2004 I published an article in the *Journal of Architectural Education*, entitled "Reimagining Walking: Four Practices," that described an approach to design rooted in bodily experience, actual space, and place. Since that time, in my role as a professor of architecture and interior design, I have thought about my own design processes and my education, and reflected on how I came to possess this particular point of view. I came to the realization that real-life encounters with good buildings and good design played a significant role. As a graduate student I had the good fortune to receive a summer travel scholarship and spent two months traveling in Europe seeing, sketching, and photographing buildings I had admired only in books and images. As a designer and a teacher I have been both interested in and concerned about the predominance of spectacle and image in the practice of design. In 2009, I taught courses about understanding architecture for non-architecture students while living in Luxembourg. I traveled extensively with my students and with my family. We walked the neighborhoods of Luxembourg City each week and traveled further afield on weekends and holidays. This book grows out of these experiences. It is both a guide to and a rumination about the connections between design education and travel; it is a manifesto for a life journey devoted to good design.

*

If you want to be an effective designer, set aside the glossy magazines, turn off your computer, and seek out first-hand encounters with beautiful design. When it comes to cities, buildings, and art, actual experience is almost always better than the virtual kind. No image can replicate Le Corbusier's Ronchamp when the light is just right, or capture the silent speech one hears on a stroll through Ian Hamilton Finlay's Little Sparta, or explain hours dissolving in Peter Zumthor's baths at Vals. That is the reason for this book: to encourage you to actively pursue direct aesthetic experience in the built environment, and to reflect upon the best reasons and ways to be a dedicated design traveler.

Traveling to learn is an integral part of the education of student architects and designers. It is vital for designers to know how to be effective design travelers, to know how to seek out and encounter places, buildings, and objects, and to develop a capacity for looking, drawing, and, above all, discerning. But to be a student is only to be "one who is studying," which means all of us, really, who if we are truly alive delight in the application of the mind to the acquisition of knowledge.

The Grand Tour

The Grand Tour is an artifact of 19th-century British Romanticism rooted in the idea that educated young persons should travel to Europe to see first-hand the legacy of Western and classical civilization, most especially through art and architecture. When you study abroad or hoist a backpack for global travel the idea of the Grand Tour is not far away.

As pursued during the British Empire, the Grand Tour was mostly the birthright of young aristocratic men, and because of this it has been disparaged, often rightly so, as an exclusive privilege of the aristocracy. Beginning amateur and would-be artists and architects took to the Grand Tour believing in their social and cultural superiority. *Dilettante*—an Italian borrowing—and its negative connotation of *a pretentious dabbling amateur*, described the behavior of many of the young men doing the Grand Tour. The sense of Western superiority, and the presumed superiority of Northern Europe, also found expression through the Grand Tour. Because of this imperialist practice, the Grand Tour *per se* is an anachronism, and the chauvinism it implies is justifiably antique. For good reason, movies, novels, histories, and academic cultural critiques all expose the pitfalls and follies of the Grand Tour. But, despite these deserved criticisms, the ideal of the Grand Tour persists because it is rooted in the idea of *self-education through direct study*.

In the age of overwhelming digital information a contemporary Grand Tour devoted primarily to exploring design affirms not only that places and buildings must be experienced in their complete physical reality to be understood, but also that learning about design depends on this experience. Experiencing the actual world takes us out of the digital one. Real stuff, after all, is what should interest designers, architects, and other students of the built environment. In this digital/image/media age it often appears that we've lost sight of the actual world. And although digital images promote the ideal of democratic access, this is more illusion than substance. Digital imagery often substitutes fragmented spectacle for experience. In the virtual landscape, the designer becomes a spectator rather than an inhabitant.

Although this book consists of words and photographs once removed from their subject, it presupposes a philosophy of architecture in which senses such as sound, temperature, time, and touch are at least as important as the visual sense. While photographs often speak of many things besides the encompassing presence of space and place—and they can easily mislead—that doesn't mean they are worthless for understanding the design of physical environments and architecture. On the contrary, in contrast to merely looking, and because of how we understand pictures, experience with actual places provides a means to integrate photographs and words. Design travel is a particularly focused way to bring together experience, narrative, and image for greater understanding of the designed environment.

The photographs in this book focus mainly on Modern and contemporary architecture in Europe. Europe is compact, it boasts an extensive public transportation network, and its post-World-War-II built environment has been shaped by well-developed public policy that values design. For these reasons, it is a model destination for the design pilgrim. It is of course possible and desirable to pursue a rigorous program of design touring both close to home and further afield on any of the world's continents. The photographs here are not meant to imply a canon or a prescriptive itinerary, rather they offer a personal collection—one example of a stepping off point for approaching, understanding, and benefiting from the experience of design travel. One of the central premises of this book is that beautiful design can be found just about anywhere if you work at it and look.

*

The Tourist

It is a commonplace to regard the tourist as a creature lower in status than a traveler. Tourism in general is often deemed escapist, consumptive, or inauthentic. You will often hear a person trying to position him or her self, not as a mere tourist, but as a traveler, and that is because—to this way of thinking—tourists are rubes, and slaves to their guidebooks. The tourist is the guy getting off the bus with the camera hanging around his neck, whereas the traveler, having hitchhiked, is lying barefoot in the sun at the top of a Tikal pyramid reading a well-thumbed copy of "Zen and the Art of Motorcycle Maintenance." Tourists are animals consecrated in the heat of marketing, half-baked narratives, and simulacra, while travelers enjoy ever more authentic experiences . . . or so this thinking goes.

But such a debate is really not helpful for the student of design. To take a side is a mistake. As a traveler, you might spend your time sitting at the café, smoking, with your Moleskine notebook in front of you, sipping pastis and cool water. A lovely and real experience, to be sure. You might wander Paris, or further afield, imagining Montmartre in the nineteen-twenties, and fantasize yourself as Ernest Hemingway or Karen Blixen . . . or Owen Wilson or Scarlett Johansen.

As thrilling as this might seem, for the student interested in design these "authentic" experiences that travelers might have miss the point—they are as contrived and created as the more predictable packaged tour (in any case, none of us can ever really escape the travel industry). Thinking of yourself favorably as a design tourist, on the other hand, you imagine you have a job to do and an itinerary to nail, places to go, and things to see. Being a design tourist means having a sense of efficiency, urgency, and organization—a definite plan for learning about design by actively looking.

It does not matter whether you call yourself a traveler or a tourist (I will use both terms here interchangeably without prejudice). But do bear in mind that when it comes to design a well-organized self-guided tour is more conducive to learning than wandering. The idea is not to pursue the marketed or even the cool experience but to identify and experience good design.

Learning to design takes years of looking. Looking precedes design. Looking is a practice of criticism, and it requires that you become a critic of design without taking on the negative connotations of the critic. To put it another way, designing is not necessarily the most important part of what designers do, but *looking* may well be. Look, and see. Look, and think. Look, and measure. Look, and discern.

Of course looking—with vision—is only one aspect of the proper appreciation of design. We understand buildings through touch, motion, haptic experience, human scale—and actual rather than virtual vision. To make the most of this holist experience requires both planning and a certain amount of perspective.

Walking and Details

There are two additional things, both related to the design process, which you may consider worthwhile to think about while touring: walking and details. They are significant parts of design learning and practice.

First of all, walking. You may do a lot of walking as a design traveler and pilgrim. I love to walk. I once walked from Georgia to my home in Maine along the Appalachian Trail, sleeping beneath the stars and living with an elegant economy. The experience informed, and perhaps instigated, thinking about walking as an architectural practice, it was a kind of Grand Tour of extended and barely differentiated space, or a pilgrimage to nature.

When it comes time to design, it makes sense to me to walk and camp in order to truly understand the cycle of time and tide and sun and the origin of place on land. We can reframe walking in terms of four practices crucial for design: *siting, measuring, reading,* and *merging.*[1] We have to re-imagine walking because when we design, when we teach and talk and think about design we have a tendency to forget the most fundamental fact—that humans stand up and walk around. This standing up and walking around gives us our "vision for designing," so to speak. Because of the stereo-optical arrangement of our eyes, we see space three-dimensionally, and what's more, movement gives us language, metaphor, and meaning-making capacity. But let's also remember that walking—our upright moving around—gives us the sense of touch, and hapticity itself—the understanding of what things will feel like before we have touched them, and hence what is known as "materiality."

These ideas about walking are a ground or basis for understanding spatial design and perception. Architecture is not altogether abstract, it is not first and foremost poetry, or explicit speech, or art, or theory, although it is all of these things at one time or another. It is more importantly the concrete and actual making of places, spaces, and objects.

Siting, measuring, reading, and merging are design practices of mud and tree and stone; they put walking to the test. When you travel, you meet design not in images in glossy magazines—or in books like this—but in actuality, not merely picking up material for quotation, but living with the idea that architecture and landscape are meaningful only in a full encounter with their details.

There are two ways to think about details in the design of buildings. Both of these ways of thinking about details are essential to the designer. One is technical: How is the building put together? How does it work? How does it manage water and other forces? The other way of thinking about details has to do with meaning: How does architecture communicate? What does it say and how does it say it? By what means does architecture move you?

Encountering buildings in the flesh makes thinking about design details far easier than doing so from a limited selection of drawings and photographs. In architecture's presence you can speculate and quiz a building about how it is doing its work. You can look from different angles and gain perspective. You can touch and measure. You can imagine a number of details and think about how they are integrated in a single aspect of the building, in a wall section "from earth to sky," for example. You can also identify outliers. You can begin to feel how a particular detail dances to a melody different from the dominant music that is frozen in the work as a whole. This is not so possible after a dissection by camera lens.

*

The Pilgrim

Many of the buildings in this book are pilgrimage sites. They are for religious, architectural, or cultural pilgrimage, or all three combined. On your journey you may find yourself thinking in terms of one or more of these categories. You may recognize yourself as a pilgrim. A pilgrim in search of Modern architecture. A pilgrim chasing the ghost of Le Corbusier. A pilgrim to the shrine of Zumthor. A pilgrim seeking the sense of sacred space. A pilgrim in pursuit of good design.

A pilgrim is a person who sets out on a journey from home on a quest in search of a lasting truth at the heart of a symbolic or metaphoric experience. The journey itself is a ritual, and the ritual a rite of passage. When you go you may have the reasonable expectation that you will be transformed. You will leave home (and take some part of home with you), you will go to a space between home and discomfort and you will find something there, and then you will return. If you are a lucky or successful pilgrim you will be surprised, and you will remember, you will understand something, and you will increase your faith.

Go to See What You Love

The purpose of architecture, according to Alain de Botton, is to show us who we might ideally hope to be. Buildings and objects speak, according to de Botton, and they speak to us as our fellow humans would speak to us. We react with first impressions to buildings and people—we feel affinity or distaste right away. We love, befriend, mistrust, despise, or ignore them. Trust your instincts, then dig deeper. This is the beginning of what is known as criticism.

I used to think that design criticism was only for people who didn't or couldn't design. I just wanted to learn to design. As a design student I believed that designing was the pinnacle activity of what we do, and that designing came out of my pencil, my hands, my eyes, and my head. That was mistaken thinking.

In actuality, design is an entirely collaborative undertaking, and being able to converse as a critic is essential to effective collaboration.

Simon Unwin, the British author of a number of books written with students in mind, including *Analysing Architecture*, and *Twenty Buildings Every Architect Should Understand*, argues for understanding architecture through drawing—plans, sections, elevations, details—especially plans. Unwin provides good counsel for learning how to be discerning: there is value in the time-honored practice of the travel sketch but, more importantly, know your subject before you go by drawing it. Develop an intimate understanding of your subject's geometries, proportional scheme, and patterns of circulation. Decode its dimensions. Understand the designer's decisions through the abstraction of drawing before you go because doing this will make your actual encounter all the more rewarding. And take your drawings with you. The connection between your hand and your eyes through drawing extends and expands to your bodily connection in actual, physical space.

In addition to knowing specific buildings you plan to visit by drawing their plans, sections, and elevations in advance, it also pays to think through carefully the full range of basic strategies designers have used in putting together buildings over the millennia. Francis D.K. Ching's perennial *Architecture: Form, Space, and Order* might give you a good encyclopedic view of possible design strategies, as does Unwin's *Analysing Architecture*, or Clark & Pause's far more abstract *Precedents in Architecture*. Make a list of ideas that seem important. Such frameworks help clarify what is tried and true, what is used over and over again, and what happens when genius gets a hold of the tools.

Thinking this way, through precedent, is important, because most of the world's pressing problems are simply too large and complex to be solved by any one individual, or even by a dedicated team. Rather than being executed by a lone genius, design is most often carried out collaboratively, and sometimes through crowd sourcing and other means made possible because of the power of computing. For designers a taxonomy of spatial design elements and strategies helps such endeavors, and it is more powerful when the designer's understanding is grounded in actuality. Studying design this way will make you a stronger collaborator.

Criticism

Criticism is about conversation. Can we begin to talk about the buildings and objects we encounter, can we articulate our responses and understandings? "It's cool," and "I like it," are the beginning of a conversation—the first inarticulate utterances on the way to something more.

If criticism begins with trying to figure out what you love, and who you ideally hope to be, it continues in a sustained way when you can begin to say what you love, what you value, and most importantly, *why*. Criticism is not just for specialist writers called critics. Criticism is for all of us. Criticism is about having a conversation with concern for the very nature and quality of the built environment on the planet we call home.

Criticism should have an earnest and noble intention about it. If it doesn't—if it is about marketing, trending, fashion, flash, and glamor, as it so often is—then in the end it is not so helpful for humanity.

Reading and writing are essential to the study of design. These conjoined activities help you to form questions, to discover what you think, and to say what you think with increasing accuracy. Imagine the ennobled humility one feels while encountering a true architecture, for example a magnificent cathedral. Such an experience is ineffable—un-utterable. Speech breaks down. You're rendered mute.

Reading and writing are therefore constant exercise . . . yoga . . . practice . . . preparation . . . for nothing less than an encounter with the divine, with the hope—a leap in expectation—of being able to survive the experience to talk about it. Talking about buildings, communication (what two or more people understand), is what matters.

What is Beauty?

Beauty is that which shall not be named. It is the thing that we do not talk about even though it is right under our noses, beneath our feet. It is the leopard in the room. It is the thing we do not speak of for fear of waking from the dead. "Beauty is the most discredited philosophical notion," writes Alexander Nehamas.

Does it strike you as odd that we, as designers, do not talk very much about beauty, even in places presumably devoted to the design of buildings, interiors, and things? Are we interested in making objects, interiors, buildings, and built environments beautiful, or not? Should we always set aside beauty in favor of technical concerns? Social issues? Architectural jargon/fashion? Functional problems? Sustainability? Or, as designers, is beauty itself an attribute of design that is worth talking about explicitly and completely?

Are you willing and interested in talking about beauty, about what is beautiful and why? Do you know how to have such a conversation? Do you have a vocabulary for it?

How might one achieve beauty in design? What is beauty's purpose? How do you know beauty when you see it?

These are questions and ideas worth entertaining, but to answer and explore them requires not shrinking from this word beauty.

There are several powerful reasons why we won't willingly venture into explicit discussion about beauty. Bringing the reasons to light, as if they were vampires, might dispel them, so here goes:

Reason one: Thought and feeling are categories opposite to one another. Emotion is inferior to reason. Beauty has to do with feeling—emotion. Case closed.

Reason two: We believe that "beauty is in the eye of the beholder," and therefore, since beauty is purely subjective, there is no point in talking about it—it comes down to preferences—we'd only be expressing our baseless opinion, to which there is no point in responding. Because our opinions are equally valid, unless we agree in our opinion there is nothing to talk about, except the fact that we disagree.

Reason three: Beauty cannot be defined. There is no precise, scientific, rational way to distinguish what is beautiful from what is not. Lacking substantial ways to precisely define beauty, it is a quality better left alone. Let us focus more on definable things, this line of thinking goes.

Reason four: Many architects and interior designers think of themselves as artists, and artists challenge conventional ways of thinking. But beautiful art is conventional art. Art should be "about" something, or it should challenge, unsettle, or disturb. Beauty is therefore unnecessary for art, art need not be beautiful; architecture and interior design therefore need not be beautiful.

Reason five: Beauty is, historically, a concern of aristocracy, or at least of the bourgeoisie. Beauty is connected with "high culture." In the United States, to take the example of one kind of experience, many people have tended to see themselves as "middle class." To speak of beauty, therefore, and to really care about beautiful places and things, is to hold yourself above others, and this is un-American. Similar prohibitions against beauty, on the grounds of snobbishness or self-superiority, exist in other cultures, except of course those cultures that are not so afraid of beauty.

There, five significant reasons why we won't talk about beauty.

Despite the conversational pitfalls outlined, achievement in the understanding of beauty is an important aspect of human progress. Beauty is consonant with human health, happiness, and prosperity, even if it is impossible to discern which came first. We should therefore seek to understand and undo ugliness at every opportunity, recognizing its human and economic cost. We should be capable of venturing a conversation about what it really means for an object, an interior, or a building to attain beauty, to *be* beautiful, and the consideration of beauty should be made a significant part of our private experience and public conversation. At the very least, in schools dedicated to design, beauty should be at the very heart of our concerns.

Know Where You Come From

If you are going to go out into the world to look at and encounter designed objects, buildings, and places, it is helpful to understand where you have come from. If you do not understand where you have come from before you go, you will certainly begin to understand as a consequence of your going. In fact, this is the single reason most often given for serious travel. You will gain perspective. Still, as part of your preparation for your trip, it might be wise to spend some time reflecting on where you have come from, rather than have such a revelation thrust upon you far from home

What sort of rooms surrounded you when you were a child? How were they furnished? Why were they furnished that way?

What did the adults who brought you into the world care about? Why did they care about these things? When you went out of doors, what did you find? Were you in the country? The city? A place with a diversity of people, or a place with people who thought they were all more or less the same? What did the world look like where you came from?

Every designer needs to reflect on where they came from. Where you came from influences everything about how you see and approach design. You cannot escape your past. Or, if you are trying to escape your past through design, there is probably a very good reason for escape. It is important to try to understand what compels, motivates, and influences you.

I grew up in the suburbs outside of Philadelphia, in a house that had been built by a prosperous building contractor, for himself, in 1895. The contractor used an unusual combination of elements in that house, in part because he could design a little as he built, and probably also because he had some parts and pieces available to him as leftovers from other jobs. It was a slightly eclectic house. When my parents took possession of the house about 1960, the widow who was leaving left all sorts of furniture and junk: a brass bed, an oak dining table, a crib made from leftover stair-rail parts. The house had behind it a carriage house with a root cellar, and in this root cellar we found sash weights, a rotted canvas tent, and short lengths of every conceivable molding profile, cut from pine, walnut, oak, and poplar.

These bits of molding were the samples and leftovers of the contractor's trade, and they became raw building materials: parts of a fort, a rabbit hutch, a tree house, and many other things. My father was a great re-purposer, too, having grown up in the Great Depression, so he made things, and sited other buildings, all around our house and barn. We had a well house, a corn crib, and a one-car garage, and each of these small buildings were arrayed around our house like satellites, and their allure beckoned us to come into the landscape—it was a landscape with buildings at a child's scale.

My parents also collected art—they lived in Chicago, then New York in the 1950s—they were progressive Modernists through and through, and the white plaster walls of the house were hung with new art. It was impossible not to look, and impossible not to learn to see, in this eclectic environment. My parents were not especially wealthy people, but in the 1950s and 60s my father was an advertising executive, first for LOOK and later LIFE magazines, and they bought art when they had extra cash: Arp, Arman, Avery, Chaissac, King, Lichtenstein, Nevelson, Porter, and many others. I grew up looking at Modern and contemporary art on an everyday basis, because I lived with it. My parents surrounded me with art. My mother wrote about art; my father also brought home his self-education in looking and seeing from the Barnes Foundation. And the pictures of LOOK and LIFE, with their powerful images, were scattered everywhere in our house.

My intention here is to explain a past. It is a curse and a blessing to have been educated from an early age to look at and through rectangles. But this was also an eclectic education in a vivid place. Everyone is influenced early in some way, and you will do well to understand what influences you and not ignore it or bury it: you can't change it, and as a traveler or a tourist you carry such childhood influences, gracefully or otherwise, as baggage.

A nineteenth-century landscape overtaken by a twentieth-century suburb, a gentlemen's farm, a stone country house made from an odd assortment of parts, old and new handmade and manufactured furnishings and objects, windows of rippled glass looking out into green, a modest collection of Modern and contemporary art—this was a mold in which I was shaped. I grew up looking at and through rectangles, at and through ten thousand things.

Take the time to reflect upon where you have come from. Write it down. It isn't something to be uncomfortable with or nostalgic for—even if you feel those feelings. It just is, and it affects everything you think and do as a designer.

*

My parents were friends with an émigré architect, my godmother, Stanisława Nowicki, who came every week to our house for dinner. This is how I experienced architecture, at the age of ten or so, at Siasia's house:

> I am walking in the space formed between a few objects: white walls, a wood floor with the color and sheen of honey, a rectangle of wool carpet, a low round molded plywood table, a vase of pussy willows, a cabinet with planes of wood, rectangles of pure color, edges of bright angled steel, a ceramic sculpture on a projecting stone ledge. I am walking toward a wall of glass, frames of steel painted white, a curtain of fine string knotted like a fishnet into squares the size of my fingertips. One of the windows is open like a door. A warm breeze moves the curtain, moves the dappled white light. I step into the narrow opening, grasp the doorframe, step over the threshold, place my sneakered foot firmly on the top step, stand to balance, and look out. It's a Saturday afternoon in spring. The steps I am standing on are part of a continuous bench, painted dark green, which runs the entire length of a broad concrete terrace. The surface of the terrace is gridded into squares. Three gently tapered columns support the ceiling over the terrace, define the edge against a flat, clipped lawn that extends way out to a tall, perfectly squared privet hedge. My parents and godmother—my Polish godmuzzer, with her clipped S's and Z's—are talking, smoking. This is gossip, *godsibb,* architecture talk. I do not understand everything that is said. The words and sentences are new, strange, rhythmic, and beautiful. I am attracted by a wedge of orange cheese, some round white crackers, small purple grapes, a clear glass pitcher of icy lemonade, a sprig of mint, droplets of light, blue-green glasses, a plain wood rectangular

tray. There is one empty green Adirondack chair for me. I sit and I'm pulled down onto the thin canvas cushion, my shoulder bones hard against the slanted flat back. The plane overhead, the wall of glass planes, the opening to the hedge and trees, these form a surrounding geometry, a real and imagined space. This, I understand now, is architecture.

The built environment shapes you. So too does the influence of adults, even though you may not fully understand what they are talking about or what they care about. So how was it for you?

Early influences, education, and what you see and touch—these are the things you must integrate in the course of a lifetime. In your lifetime you will see and experience more buildings and spaces than you ever design, and together with your childhood experiences and your formal education, you will bring your travel experiences to your work. To be a design tourist it is helpful to know where you've come from so that you can know what baggage you are carrying as you go, what filters your eyeglasses contain, what you've got buried, and what you know that you know.

The most important reason for design travel is that it develops one's capacity for criticism and the discernment of beauty, and hence one's capacity for design. Design is about making decisions within an unlimited universe of possibilities. And while ignorance might limit the number of possibilities, it does nothing for the design student's capacity for discerning. So . . . expand: walk and look, touch and listen, read and write, and converse.

Design travel is about looking out into the world and setting your sights on buildings and places you suspect you will admire, on architecture with some reasonable claim to quality, on things worth seeing. It is also about reflecting on who we might ideally be (not in a self-involved, individual, feel-good sense, or in a professional sense, but in a collective and social sense). Design travel requires perceiving beauty and embracing criticism, knowing where you are going and where you have come from. It's about using your entire body to understand design; it's about looking, touching, lingering, and drawing. Even if the activity seems overly privileged and consumptive, design travel is about caring for the beauty of the world, the usefulness of design, and our common humanity.

Logistics

Being a design tourist requires knowing what you are looking for. Develop an itinerary, figure out where to go and why, study the target subject, find out in advance when and how to visit a particular building or place.

Fortunately, we have the Internet and the Web, and with a little discernment and persistence, you can easily find touring information by going online. There is an abundance of information: Great Buildings Online presents "one thousand classics . . . around the world and across history." Two websites worth looking at are Galinsky and MiMoa. Galinsky is much narrower in its scope, and more carefully edited. MiMoa is open-source, which means it is inconsistent, but growing. These two websites are biased toward Modern and contemporary architecture tourism—good places for designers to go to learn about present and recent past design (also see the resources section of this book).

Destinations

As with books, if you hear a designer or a building mentioned three times (or maybe only once) get the spelling, write it down, and do some research. Go look it up. Read the syllabus or the newspaper, take note of the slides—see who or what others have thought worth mentioning.

Browse the library. Not only the virtual one, but the actual one. Go on a hunt. Ask a librarian to help find designers and designs worth seeking. Ask a professor or colleague. Read one of the guides to contemporary global architecture, or to the architecture of Chicago, Beijing, or Rotterdam. Make and maintain a list of buildings and designers. But remember that this is your list—make it how you want it—be wary of the notion that there is a canon of buildings you must see. Plan on seeing what you want to see.

Should you go with a friend, or go it alone?

The advantage of going with a friend is that you may often have someone to talk to about what you like and why, if you find talking about what you see helpful to understanding. But choose your friends wisely. That they should be fun to be around goes without saying. Choose someone who likes to think and talk and look, maybe even someone who you believe is smarter than you. Also, if traveling by car, choose someone who is a good driver or a good navigator; it's important to have two brains and a GPS behind the windshield when driving in unknown territory in a foreign land. Second and third languages also don't hurt.

On the other hand, if you go alone you can go exactly where you want, and stay as long as you like, and change your itinerary on a whim. You'll have more freedom, if that is important to you. In the solitude of your own thoughts and perceptions, you may well be able to reflect more deeply on the beauty of the places you encounter.

Don't Forget About Art

Global cultural life is a living, breathing, always changing situation, and you need to think beyond buildings devoid of the people and institutions that are housed within them. It is worth looking to see what's on. Particularly worthwhile art exhibitions are a once in a decade, or even a once in a lifetime experience. Some buildings—such as those built for exhibitions—are once in forever, built and then recycled, and seeing them in the flesh while they are up is important because they often embody significant contemporary ideas. Take the time to participate in cultural life as a citizen to reflect on the significant differences between art, architecture, design, and craft.

The museum, though a problematic idea, has nevertheless been a site of architectural discourse in the last two or three decades, and you could make a worthwhile global tour of museums alone. Art museums have another advantage for the design traveler—they are by definition public—places specifically designed for looking—it is possible to actually see them inside and out at a reasonable pace, which means getting to know them thoroughly, deeply, and well.

The Fabric of Cities

While you are traveling it pays to get to know the cities you are encountering as a whole. Make sure you do some background reading. Look especially for non-standard and up-to-the-minute sources that might give some suggestions for understanding changing neighborhoods. Ask locals. Buy an unlimited public transit pass and ride across or around town into areas not normally part of the tourist itinerary—this works especially well above ground in the front or the back of the bus.

Transportation

Planes, trains, or automobiles. Each mode of transportation will affect the experience of looking. Travelling exclusively by plane and train, as romantic and traveller-worthy as it is, means seeing a lot of train stations and airports, but it also means missing some of the details that define a place. It also sometimes takes more time. Cars and bicycles can be helpful in many places and they provide an intimate encounter with the landscape and many opportunities for getting lost. In any case, planning transportation is essential: use a good map.

*

We need to act on global carbon emissions urgently. There are consequences to getting on airplanes and driving cars, but making more beauty is also part of the solution to environmental problems. With respect to sustainability, we need to think as much about the aesthetics of design as the mechanics of carbon-mitigating technology—how people feel and breath and live in a building, and how the spirit might soar. David Orr has said that we need to make ourselves *worthy of being sustained.* Making the world more beautiful is part of that worthiness.

Still, in spite of the far away images in this little book, you could instead choose to tour closer to home, and use your own two feet or a bicycle, and make opportunities to see buildings without making a special, carbon intensive trip.

Endnotes

[1]   Ben Jacks, "Reimagining Walking: Four Practices," *Journal of Architectural Education*, (Boston: MIT Press for the Association of Collegiate Schools of Architecture) 57:3, February, 2004, 5-9.

Suggested Readings

Michael Benedikt, *For an Architecture of Reality,* (New York: Lumen Books, 1987).

Kent C. Bloomer and Charles W. Moore, *Body, Memory, & Architecture,* (New Haven: Yale University Press, 1977).

Alain de Botton, *The Architecture of Happiness,* (New York: Pantheon Books, 2006).

Alain de Botton, *The Art of Travel,* (New York: Vintage, 2002).

Gerardo Brown-Manrique, *The Ticino Guide,* (New York: Princeton Architectural Press, 1989).

Deborah Gans, *The Le Corbusier Guide,* (New York: Princeton Architectural Press, 2006).

J.W. Goethe, *Italian Journey* [1786-1788], tr. W.H.Auden & Elizabeth Mayer, (New York: Penguin, 1962).

Lisa Heschong, *Thermal Delight in Architecture,* (Cambridge, MA: MIT Press, 1979).

J. B. Jackson, *Discovering the Vernacular Landscape,* (New Haven: Yale University Press, 1986).

Robert Kahn & Tim Adams (eds.), *City Secrets London: The Essential Insider's Guide,* (New York: Fang Duff Kahn, 2011).

Sergio Los, *Carlo Scarpa: An Architectural Guide,* (Verona: Arsenale Editrice, 2006).

Robert McCarter, *Carlo Scarpa,* (New York: Phaidon Press, 2013).

Juhani Pallasmaa, *The Eyes of the Skin,* (Chichester, UK: Wiley, 2005).

Steven Park, *Le Corbusier Redrawn: The Houses,* (New York: Princeton Architectural Press, 2012).

Steen Eiler Rasmussen, *Experiencing Architecture,* (Cambridge, MA: MIT Press, 1962).

Jessie Sheeler & Andrew Lawson, *Little Sparta: The Garden of Ian Hamilton Finlay,* (London: Frances Lincoln, 2003).

Rebecca Solnit, *Wanderlust: a History of Walking,* (New York: Peguin, 2001).

Suggested Readings cont.

Philip Trager & Vincent Scully, *The Villas of Palladio,* (New York: New York Graphic Society, 1986).

Michael Trencher, *The Alvar Aalto Guide,* (New York: Princeton Architectural Press, 1996).

Simon Unwin, *Analysing Architecture,* (New York: Routledge, 2014).

Simon Unwin, *Twenty Buildings Every Architect Should Understand,* (New York: Routledge, 2010).

Lutz Windhöfel, *Architectural Guide Basel: New Buildings in the Trinational City since 1980,* (Basel, Birkhäuser, 2008).

Thomas Durisch (ed), Peter Zumthor, *Peter Zumthor: Buildings and Projects, 1985-2013,* (Zürich: Scheidegger and Spiess, 2014).

Peter Zumthor, *Atmospheres,* (Basel, Birkhäuser, 2006).

Photographs

I took the photographs in this book on multiple trips with my young family, with students, and alone. As such, the pictures are divided into sections by city or region, but this is only to have some degree of organization. This collection of photographs is a personal and idiosyncratic reflection. I hope you enjoy the pictures, but do your own research and build your own tours around what interests you.

For me, the photograph is an object in its own right. It arises from an instantaneous and intuitive exploration. I take photographs in part to remember—not that I do not also have actual memories, but a photograph is a different kind of remembering, and a hard drive full of them a special kind of memory structure. It involves aesthetic experience: seeing, responding, and composing. If there is something like artistic expression in a photograph it seems to me that expression comes from the world of things.

Organizing and identifying the places in the photographs I was reminded of the virtuality that has overtaken daily experience because of digital pictures: one can take a virtual tour of Woodland Cemetery online, for instance, or ride the Zeche Zollverein escalator on YouTube ("ride," of course, is an overstatement). Nevertheless, this virtuality and unreality is a significant aspect of contemporary life. I want to try to understand it and put it in its proper place.

Scotland & London

Ian Hamilton Finlay and Sue Finlay created the garden, Little Sparta, over decades; Peter Zumthor and Piet Oudolf's secret garden, the 2011 Serpentine Museum Pavilion, lasted just five months. Both are a testament to the ephemeral and durable nature of beauty (the "hard core of beauty," as Zumthor has written).

*

On one trip on my own, without family, I went to Little Sparta, then walked the West Highland Way, climbed Ben Nevis, and took the night train back to London. The landscape from the observation car was pure magic—a trip to Hogwart's—and a great perspective from which to see the city afresh.

*

I am a Phillippe Starck fan, not because his work is beautiful, but rather because his work is about changing the human relationship to designed objects and moving people more universally toward one another, which is a surprising thing from a rock-star designer.

52

53

Paris

On my first trip to Paris, when I was in college, I discovered the memorial to those deported from France to the Nazi concentration camps. On Île de la Cité walk around behind Notre Dame and find your way down to water level.

*

In Paris see the sights, of course, and walk the gardens, and eat, and look at art. But it is also worthwhile to take some time to think about Le Corbusier, arguably the most influential architect of the 20th century, for good and ill: *what if* his vision for Paris had been realized?

*

Outside Paris, in Poissy, the iconic Villa Savoye, completed in 1929, had the impact on architecture of a manifesto. It included Le Corbusier's "Five Points," and embodied the revolutionary idea that "the house is a machine for living."

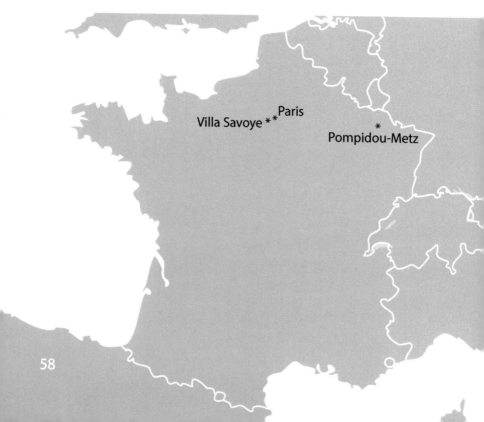

Gerrit Rietveld designed the house that epitomizes *De Stijl*, for his client Truus Schröder and her three children, but Mrs. Schröder supplied the truly radical vision. The house is a UNESCO world heritage site, as are some other places in this book. On a guided tour, when the gloved and slippered docent moves the walls on the second floor as Truus Schröder wished them to be, and when he swings open the corner window at the ledge where the children studied, the design of the world becomes clear. It is, simply, breathtaking. Even more so if you can imagine "the plain of Flanders" that existed there when the house was first built.

*

The Dutch have been in the forefront of architecture/ urban design/ landscape/ design for a number of years, and there is much to see that is new, but the Hoge-Veluwe National Park, near Arnhem, Netherlands is an older, more established, but ever-evolving gem. You can ride a borrowed bicycle through the park to the Kröller-Müller Museum, which has the second largest collection of Van Goghs, and one of the largest outdoor sculpture gardens in Europe.

*

Not among my photographs here is the Rietveld sculpture pavilion at Kröller-Müller, which was decrepit the first time I saw it, dismantled the second, and is now perfectly restored.

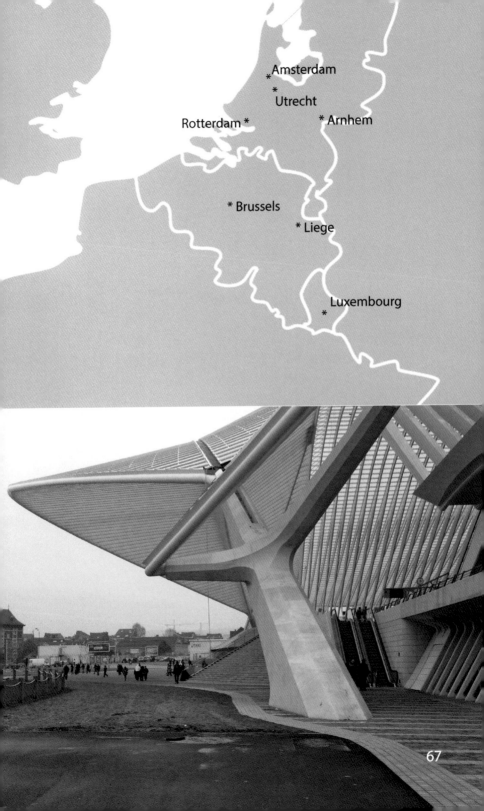

Scandinavia

A world design leader, Denmark has added a number of new buildings to Copenhagen Harbor since I was last there, which is why you will want to build your Scandinavian tour from your own fresh research.

*

In Copenhagen, we slept in a floating hotel, walked the Old Town's streets, toured the harbor, and rattled along on the wooden roller coaster in Tivoli Gardens.

*

Outside of Stockholm the Woodland Cemetery is well known as a spiritual landscape that affects the walker with shifting perceptions and moods. Walk with patience, and time on your side.

In my photograph the Woodland Chapel interior appears like a dollhouse, and it startles me every time I see it.

*

My photographs of Aalto are lost to the long-ago world of Kodachrome slides, but not to memory and, for me, there is a whole world yet to explore north of Oslo, Copenhagen, and Helsinki. In travel, I think, there is always another place to live for.

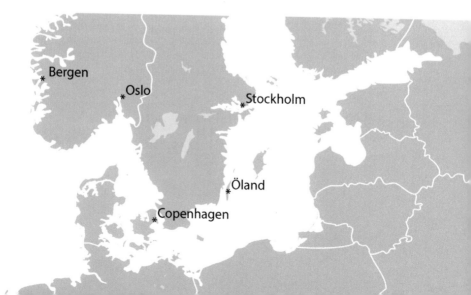

Germany

The Landscape Park at Duisberg North, and the Zollverein Coal Mine complex in Essen, Germany, are both part of the European Route of Industrial Heritage. They have been converted, rather than scrapped and buried, so that we might have better perspective about our industrial past and present. For obvious reasons, this region was heavily bombed during the Second World War.

*

Peter Zumthor has been called "a watchmaker," or more generously, an architect's architect. I love his work, and not because of its outward appearance, though I love that too, but rather because of the consonance between his writing, work process, and the buildings. That kind of integrity is worth following.

The stories behind, and the connections between, Zumthor's Kolumba Museum and the Bruder Klaus chapel, are rich and deep and beautiful. These buildings, as I see things, are worth pilgrimage in many seasons.

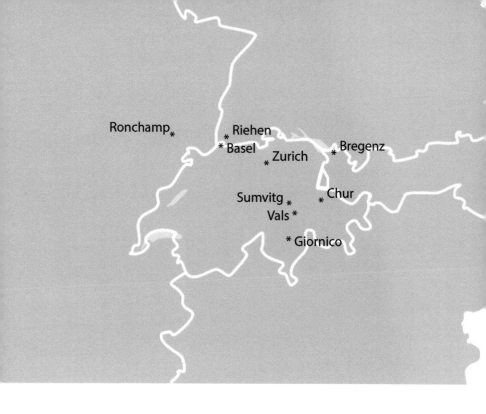

Switzerland (and Ronchamp, France)

Outside of Basel in Weil am Rhein, Germany, Vitra, the international furniture company, continues to build a Disneyland of architecture. No wonder, since Frank Gehry supplied Vitra's owners with the initial idea, straight from LA. Nearby, on the Swiss side of the border, the Beyeler Foundation houses its major collection of Modern art and tribal sculptures from Africa, Oceania, and Alaska in an exceptional and serene building by Renzo Piano, the master of the technically perfect top-lit gallery space. And in and around Basel there is much more architecture to see from the so-called "Swiss School."

*

Le Corbusier's Chapel of Notre Dame du Haut in Ronchamp, France, is also easily reached from Basel by car or bus. A site of pilgrimage for design tourists and the faithful alike, Ronchamp rewards the slow and patient traveler. I have stayed to watch the light change, attend Mass, and engage in conversation with one of the Sister's Clare. Iconic, and great, Ronchamp is one of the most important buildings of the twentieth century. And Renzo Piano's addition did not ruin it after all.

∗

The thermal baths at Vals remind me that architecture is best when it engages multiple senses, when it just is rather than is about something, when what it looks like is less important than how it feels, how it performs, and how you perform in it. The baths return me to my self, to water and stone, to presence and immensity. Encountering this architecture can change you.

You reach the Vals valley from Chur by car, or train and post bus, on a dizzying mountain climb. It takes some effort to get there, which only makes it more worthwhile.

∗

In the Italian-speaking Canton of Ticino, I especially wanted to visit Peter Märkli's, "La Congiunta" in Giornico, which houses sculpture by Hans Josephsohn. You pick up the key at a bar in the village, then walk across and along the river in pilgrimage to the shrine to Märkli's teacher.

97

105

110

115

118

LUDEIILSEGN
ERTSCHIELE
TIARALUDEIIL
SEGNERTUTTAS
CREATIRASLU
DEIILSEGNER
TUTTASNAZIUNS
CAPLUTTADA
SOGNBENEDETG
BENEDIDAILS
VENTGATSCHUN
DASEITEMBER
MELUNOVESCH
IENOTCONIOTG

123

124

La Tourette

We went to La Tourette on a long drive to Italy in December. Though we knew we were near, in the town of L'Arbresle, our paper maps and GPS were not cooperating to show us the rest of the way, so I pulled the car into a municipal lot with a large permanent map placard showing visitor's information. There was a young man standing there in the frosty air, also looking at the map. I guessed he was an architecture student also looking for La Tourette, so I offered him a ride, which he accepted indifferently. His name was Yoske, from Japan. He squeezed into the back seat with our children, which freaked them out. His English was poor, and our Japanese non-existent, so we did not have much conversation driving the rest of the way to La Tourette, but I hoped he was happy for the lift. Pilgrims like to be pilgrims together.

*

I have in mind a future tour that would go from Ronchamp, to La Tourette, to Firminy, to the Lacoste Winery, to Le Corbusier's Cabin, and the newly restored Villa E-1027 by Eileen Gray.

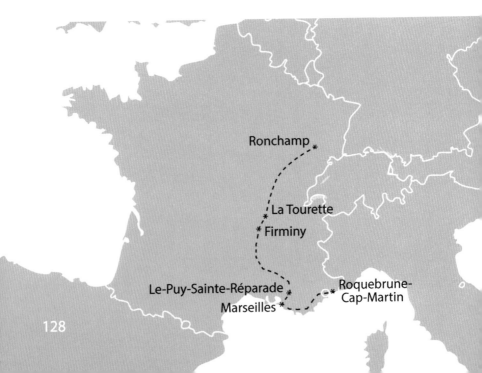

Italy

In the Veneto, you could spend months exploring Palladio, arguably the most influential architect of all time, or you could pursue Carlo Scarpa, one of the most misunderstood. Each would richly reward you.

*

In Venice we experienced *acqua alta* three times on our short trip, and got to know the front desk clerk at our hotel because of his diligence with the floodgate and the portable pump at the front door, and the loan of rubber boots. Yes, the Calatrava bridge is dangerously slippery when wet.

*

We spent one winter holiday in Florence, which offered a refreshing point of view for one of the most visited and touristed Italian cities.

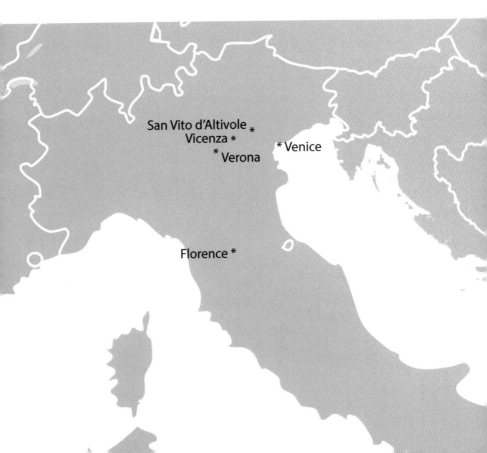

San Vito d'Altivole *
Vicenza *
* Verona
* Venice

Florence *

CHANGING
PLACE
CHANGING
TIME
CHANGING
THOUGHTS
CHANGING
FUTURE"

133

Prague

We flew to Prague from Paris on a discount airline that packs you in practically standing up, and uses obscure airports. We arrived at our hotel late at night, which seemed a fitting way to re-visit Kafka's land. It is an Old World city, at least in feeling, and therefore provides a nice contrast for the Modern and contemporary architecture tourist. There are relatively few new buildings near the old center—Frank Gehry and Vladimir Milunic's "Fred and Ginger" building is a well known exception.

There is quietude, and a density of beautiful detail, in Prague, that feels unique among European cities I have visited.

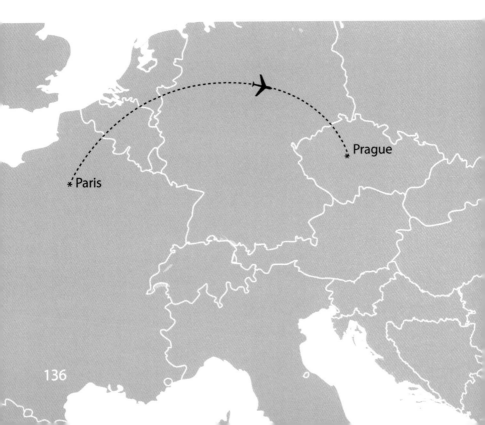

141

Spain

In 2010 *Vanity Fair* magazine asked ninety of the world's leading architects, teachers, and critics to name the five most important buildings since 1980. The results, from fifty-two experts, were decisive, and Frank Gehry's Guggenheim Museum Bilbao led the list by a factor of three. Among the many aspects of the building's influence is the so-called *Bilbao effect*—the idea that a major project by a star architect can jumpstart the economy of a city or region. But the building is much more than that implies—as the *VF* article points out, Philip Johnson called it "the greatest building of our time." You might disagree with that exclamation, but Guggenheim Bilbao is so worth experiencing for yourself, as is the permanent installation of monumental works by Richard Serra housed in an airplane hanger-sized hall.

*

In San Sebastian, grappling with city, stone, and thundering surf, is Eduardo Chilleda's massive sculpture Peine del Viento ("Wind Comb"), which makes a worthy introduction to this Basque artist's body of work, examples of which are housed nearby at Chilleda Leku.

*

Our journey in Spain was a two-way trip from Barcelona in a rented car, after several days of eating tapas, looking at Joan Miró, and touring Gaudi, though I remember it falsely as a ferocious drive from Bilbao with a stay in the cold, arid middle at the Hotel Aire de Bardenas, where stacked melon crates buffer the wind. Culminating the journey was a trip to Mies van der Rohe's reconstructed masterpiece, the Barcelona Pavilion, which speaks elegantly for itself.

143

149

Strategic Tips

• Keep a text file list (or bookmark) of what you find interesting from the very beginning rather than counting on being able to find your way back to favorite sites later.

• Consider your mode of travel (bicycle, car, bus, train) and build a realistic itinerary at a pace that feels right to you; consider that you might modify it once you are on the road.

• Use *Mappy* (the European equivalent of *MapQuest*) to estimate distances and plan routes between individual sites.

• Use *Rome2Rio* to "discover how to get anywhere by plane, train, bus, ferry and automobile."

• For train travel, the timetable of Deutsche Bahn (DB)— the German National Railways—covers all of Europe including the UK, and it is wise to consider what the train can and cannot do for your itinerary in advance rather than winging it.

• Use an app such as *WorldMate*, *TripCase*, or *TripIt* to organize your trip, or simply create a detailed itinerary (you might as well use the 24-hour clock format for convenience) with phone numbers for printing out, with tickets, reservations, etc.

Major Online Sources for Design Travelers
MIMOA
www.mimoa.eu
Extensive, user-generated Modern and contemporary
     architecture guide with multiple tools and features.
     MIMOA recently exceeded 30,000 registered users.

Galinsky
www.galinsky.com
Contributor-driven Modern and contemporary architecture
guide with multiple tools and features.

Great Buildings Collection Online
www.greatbuildings.com
Selected by the editors of Architecture Week. A thousand
buildings around the world and across history, with
photographs and drawings, and 3D building models.

arch daily
www.archdaily.com
"The world's most visited architecture website" offers numerous
City Guides.

e-architect
www.e-architect.co.uk
Edited by a UK-based editorial team, e-architect's global
collection of buildings is searchable by architect, building,
city. In addition, e-architect offers city walking tours
through a global network of guides in Europe, Asia, and
the Americas.

Architizer
A social media platform launched in 2009, Architizer now
includes over 50,000 recent architecture and design
projects uploaded by designers, and the products used to
build them.

Dezeen
This London based architecture and design magazine offers
high-quality journalism, including stories about cutting-
edge ideas and projects, and industry news.

Resources from Architecture Publishers

Besides publishing print guides, some of these publishers provide online services, for example, the downloadable apps from PHAIDON, including 70 Wallpaper* City Guide apps for Amsterdam to Zurich

www.phaidon.com/apps/wallpaper-city-guides/
PHAIDON
www.phaidon.com

DOM publishers
www.dom-publishers.com/en
Publishers of Architectural guides to Venice, Riga, Brazil, Delhi, Hong Kong, Japan, Helsinki, Taiwan, Pyongyang, Tokyo

Lars Müller Publishers
www.lars-mueller-publishers.com/en

Librairie Didier Lecointre & Dominique Drouet
19th & 20th century architecture, civil engineering and decorative arts

010 Publishers
www.010.nl
Dutch publisher of architecture and design

Hugh Pagan Limited
www.hughpagan.com
Rare and out-of-print books and periodicals in the field of architecture and architectural history

Princeton Architectural Press
www.papress.com
Architecture, graphic design and landscape architecture

a+t architecture publishers
www.aplust.net/idioma/en

Thames & Hudson
www.thamesandhudson.com

Architecture & Design Institutions and Museums

Amsterdam:
Architectuurcentrum Amsterdam
www.arcam.nl

Basel:
Swiss Architecture Museum
www.sam-basel.org/en

Berlin:
Architecture Forum Aedes
www.aedes-arc.de/sixcms/detail.php?template_id=2122

Bauhaus Archive
www.bauhaus.de/en/

German Architecture Center-DAZ
www.daz.de/daz/home/en/

Bordeaux
Architecture Center Arc en Rêve
www.arcenreve.com/Pages/pages.html

Bristol:
The Architecture Centre
www.architecturecentre.co.uk/home

Brussels:
CIVA: Centre International pour la Ville, l'Architecture et la Paysage (International Center for City, Architecture & Landscape)
www.civa.be

Copenhagen:
Danish Architecture Centre
www.dac.dk/en/front-page/

Dessau:
Bauhaus Dessau
www.bauhaus-dessau.de/english/home.html

Frankfurt am Main:
German Architecture Museum-DAM
www.dam-online.de/

Ghent:
Design Museum Gent
www.designmuseumgent.be/eng/collections.php

Helsinki:
Architecture Information Centre Finland
www.archinfo.fi/english/finnisharchitecture.fi
Museum of Finnish Architecture
www.mfa.fi/frontpage

Istanbul:
Istanbul Design Centre
www.istanbuldesigncenter.org/

Jyväskyla:
Alvar Aalto Museum
www.alvaraalto.fi/index_en.htm

London:
Design Museum
www.designmuseum.org/

NLA: London's Centre for the Built Environment
www.newlondonarchitecture.org

Munich:
The A. M.: Architecture Museum Technical University
Munich
www.architekturmuseum.de/en/home/

Orléans:
The Turbulences-FRAC Centre
www.frac-centre.fr/_en/

Oslo:
DogA-The Norwegian Centre for Design and Architecture
www.doga.no/in-english
National Museum of Art, Architecture, and Design

Paris:
Le Pavillon de l'Arsenal
(the centre for urban planning and architecture of Paris)
www.pavillon-arsenal.com/en/home.php

Fondation Le Corbusier
www.fondationlecorbusier.fr/corbuweb/morpheus.
aspx?sysName=home&sysLanguage=en-en&sysInfos=1

Rotterdam:
Het Niewe Institute/ The New Institute
www.hetnieuweinstituut.nl/en

Stockholm:
Swedish Centre for Architecture and Design
www.arkdes.se

Weil am Rhein (Germany, but close to Basel):
Vitra Design Museum
www.design-museum.de/en/information.html

Zurich:
Museum of Design
www.museum-gestaltung.ch/en/exhibitions/

Research

Shannon Van Kirk*

A few decades ago, when planning a trip abroad, my husband and I would unroll a large laminated map on the dining room table showing the part of the world we planned to visit. We would put a red dot on the arrival airport and start plotting routes. Usually we had an idea of some of our destinations—fascinating buildings: C. R. Mackintosh's Glasgow School of Art or the Art Nouveau "Hatrack"; pilgrimage sites: Castlerigg and Stonehenge; and more up to the minute interests such as the Glastonbury, Copredy, and Big Chill music festivals.

We would pore over travel guides, the Travel sections of the NY Times or the LA Times. As the weeks and months progressed toward our departure date, we would jot down interesting locales mentioned in our fiction reading and our geographically-focused non-fiction. We would ask our well-traveled friends for tips.

Adventures seemed to invent themselves. One day while studying our map, I noticed thin red lines going from a Scottish village called Stranraer over the North Channel to another small town, Larne, in Northern Ireland. Ferry routes, of course. On the way, the ferry passed very near the island called Ailsa Craig, where I knew the granite for curling stones was quarried—a pilgrimage of sorts for *this* curling fan. We did not hesitate to add this side trip. We decided we would drive from Larne to Belfast, then south through the Ards Peninsula where Bob, the family ornithologist, could seek migrating swans in Strangford Lough, and so down to Dublin and Dun Laoghaire, where another ferry would take us over the Irish Sea to Wales.

Slowly our itinerary took visible shape on our dining room table. We made phone calls, sent letters of inquiry via snail mail, purchased tickets from a travel agent—no e-commerce at that time—and our lists slowly grew longer. From tiny red lines on a map to a wonderful travel adventure: the perfect marriage of planning and serendipity.

Travel research is still full of exciting discoveries, but a trip like the one just described can be planned in hours or a few days— if done properly—instead of months of following leads. Not that there is usually a rush, but getting instant answers via the web about accommodations, tickets, local festivals, opening times of buildings, local maps, and the availability of tours and car rentals leaves more time for dreaming. Now almost everything can be booked and purchased online, eliminating unnecessary waiting.

But internet research is often hit-or-miss. The real problem with searching the web is that you will always find something. Good, bad, or indifferent, your browser will try to make you happy and, given that Google is in the business of serving ads, to sell you things, by showing you commercial links—sometimes thousands of them. How much more efficient and accurate would it be if you'd prepare a search strategy in advance in order to exercise a little control over your excessively compliant browser?

Here is the good news: the more frequently you perform targeted searches, the better you get at it. The key to the system is to have a handful of relevant web addresses and enough strategic keywords to find what you need and then some more of what you need. Make it a habit to read the address of each link before you click it so you can discern the nature of the suggested source: authoritative institution (Danish Architecture Centre), blog (www.lifeofanarchitect.com), travel guide, Facebook page, and so on. Quickly, patterns will emerge and you will become an expert searcher.

Effective Web Research

As noted, some browser searches might produce useful results, especially since they now accept natural language, for example, *best and most exciting new buildings in London*. This search actually produces some interesting results; but you can often do better by using an effective search strategy when you want to be more focused. This calls for the use of *keyword sets.* Some examples:

Paris architecture center
Result: Le Pavillon de l'Arsenal: Architecture Centre Paris
www.pavillon-arsenal.com/en/home.php

London architecture center
Result: New London Architecture: London's Centre for the Built Environment
www.newlondonarchitecture.org

The same is true for tours. Search phrases:
London architecture tour or *London modern architecture tour*

The search phrases are spare and targeted, no extraneous words, no *the*, *a*, or *an*.

Search for individual architects the same way. Their names are your keywords.

Practice searching with your own keywords, based on your own interests and destinations, type of architecture, or even a particular concept. All of these are possible keywords. Just remember to keep your searches specific, asking for only what you need in order to cause the browser to locate the most relevant links. It is worth remembering that Google usually places paid ads at the top of search results—at least they are now labeled as ads, so scroll down if you want less biased results.

Scholarly Resources

If you have access to a college or university library, there is an entirely different set of resources available to you. Scholarly databases are usually discipline-specific, covering related topics both broadly and deeply. These databases are not available to everyone because they are proprietary products for which university libraries pay licensing fees based on the number of students enrolled in the institution. To access these resources, you must have permission to visit the library, or have a university affiliation, which grants you both onsite and remote access.

What makes these databases so valuable (and their licenses so expensive), is that most of them now supply the full text of the articles discovered by the search. This requires agreements between the journal publishers and the aggregators— vendors—of the databases. Costs are passed on to the libraries that supply the databases for their patrons. Some examples of scholarly Architecture databases are:

JSTOR: the Art, Art History & Architecture Discipline Collection
Art & Architecture Complete
Art and Architecture Images

Art Full Text
Art Index Retrospective
Avery Index to Architectural Periodicals

Like ordinary web browsers, these databases are best searched using keywords. The difference is that you will not use generic words such as *architecture*, because in a database devoted to architecture, this search word is so prevalent that it will cause the database to return thousands of articles. Instead, your searches should be more targeted and specific: an architect's name, the name of a specific building, or a movement, e.g. Georgian, Beaux Arts, Art Nouveau, Mid-century Modern, Gothic, Sustainable, Passive House, etc.

You will also notice that scholarly databases offer Boolean searching, a mathematical logic system in which your keywords are connected to the operators (words) *and, or,* or *not.* These terms are supplied; you will not type them as part of your search. You enter keywords into search boxes connected by the Boolean operators that you select. These search strategies will either broaden or narrow your search results.

OR broadens your search results: *building* OR *structure* OR *edifice* will return all items with any of these three keywords.

NOT narrows your search results: *pavilion* NOT *kiosk* will return all items containing the word pavilion but not items containing the word kiosk.

AND narrows your search results, sometimes dramatically: *serra* AND *sculpture* AND *qatar* will return only items that contain all three words, not just one or two of them. This term is useful when you want a very focused search (see examples below).

Sample searches that will yield targeted results. Note that keyword searching is case neutral:

calatrava AND *bridges*

jeppe hein AND *water pavilion*

norman foster AND *lords media centre*

If you have practiced being a thoughtful web searcher, you should feel entirely comfortable with the more focused and systematic searches usually required in scholarly databases. And if in doubt, feel free to ask your university librarian for help: that is what we are there for.

*Shannon Van Kirk, former colleague and head of the Wertz Art & Architecture Library at Miami University, earned her Master of Library and Information Studies degree from the University of Alabama.

Photographs

(all photographs are by the author)

7: Louvre Pyramid, Louvre Museum, I.M. Pei, Paris

9: Villa Savoye, Le Corbusier, Poissy, France

13: Bruder Klaus Chapel, Peter Zumthor, Mechernich, Germany

16: Bregenz Art Museum, Peter Zumthor, Bregenz, Austria

19: Vitra Warehouse, Alvaro Siza, Weil am Rhein, Germany

21: Vitra Fire Station, Zaha Hadid, Weil am Rhein, Germany

24: Notre Dame du Haut, Le Corbusier, Ronchamp, France

28, 28: St. Benedikt Chapel, Peter Zumthor, Sumvitg, Switzerland

31: La Tourette, Le Corbusier, Eveux, France

33: Chiesa di San Giovanni Battista, Mario Botta, Mogno, Switzerland

35: River Thames, London

41, 42, 43 (top): "Little Sparta," Ian Hamilton Finlay, Dunsyre, Scotland

43 (middle, bottom): Scottish Parliament, Enric Miralles, Edinburgh, Scotland

44: Phillipe Starck, St. Martin's Lane Hotel, London

45 (top left): Anish Kapoor exhibition, Royal Academy of Fine Arts, London

45, 46: Serpentine Gallery Pavilion 2011, Peter Zumthor (building) & Piet Oudolf (garden), London

47 (top): Millennium Bridge, Arup/Foster & Partners/Anthony Caro, London

47 (bottom): Tate Modern, Herzog & de Meuron, London

48 (top left): Picadilly Circus, London

48 (top right): Phillipe Starck, St. Martin's Lane Hotel, London

48 (top right lower, middle left): graffiti near Whitechapel

48 (middle right): Whitechapel Gallery, London

48 (bottom left): Fieldgate Street (foreground), Royal London Hospital (background), London

48 (bottom right): Nido Spitalfields, TP Bennett Architects, London

49: "The Gherkin," 30 St. Mary Axe, Norman Foster, London

50 (top left, middle right): "The Cheesegrater," 122 Leadenhall Street, Richard Rogers, London

50 (top right, middle left): Lloyds of London, Richard Rogers, London

50 (bottom): street sign, Bankside, London
51 (top, middle): Lloyds Register, Richard Rogers, London
51 (bottom left): Tower Bridge, John Wolfe Barry and Horace Jones, London
51 (bottom right): Jubilee Line Extension, London
52-57: Jubilee Line Extension, London
57 (bottom): Thames skyline, London
59 (top left): Mama Restaurant, Mama Shelter Hotel, Phillippe Starck, Paris
59 (top right): Cartier Foundation for Contemporary Art, Jean Nouvel, Paris
59 (middle): billboard photograph, exhibition 'Petite Planete': Martin Paar, Jeu de Paume Gallery, Paris
59 (bottom): Pyramid, The Louvre Museum, I.M. Pei, Paris
60 (top): Pompidou Center, Piano & Rogers, Paris
60 (bottom): *Les Deux Plateaux,* "Buren's Columns," Palais Royal, Daniel Buren, Paris
61: Villa La Roche, Le Corbusier, Paris
62, 63, 64 (top): Villa Savoye, Le Corbusier, Poissy, France
64 (bottom), 65: Pompidou Center, Shigeru Ban, Metz, France
67 (bottom), 68 (top left): Liège-Guillemins Train Station, Santiago Calatrava, Liège, Belgium
68 (top right): Brussels, Belgium
68 (lower top left): Christian de Portzamparc, Hergé Museum, Louvain la Neuve, Belgium
68 (middle left): Stedelijk Museum, Benthem Crouwel, Amsterdam
68 (middle right): 1928 Olympic Stadium, Jan Wils, Amsterdam, Netherlands
68 (bottom left): Ittala, Utrecht, Netherlands
68 (bottom right): Rietveld-Schröder House, Gerrit Rietveld/Truus Schröder, Utrecht, Netherlands
69 (top): Cube Houses, Piet Blom, Rotterdam, Netherlands
69 (middle left): Netherlands Architecture Institute, Jo Coenen, Rotterdam, Netherlands
69 (middle right): entry lodge, MVRDV, Hoge-Veluwe National Park, Otterlo, Netherlands
69 (bottom): *Jardin d'émail,* Jean Dubuffet, Kröller-Müller Museum, Otterlo, Netherlands

70 (top): Kröller-Müller Museum, Otterlo, Netherlands
70 (middle): *Two adjacent pavilions*, Dan Graham, Kröller-Müller Museum, Otterlo, Netherlands
70 (bottom): Kröller-Müller Museum, Otterlo, Netherlands
71 (top left): sculpture pavilion, Aldo van Eyck, Kröller-Müller Museum, Otterlo, Netherlands
71 (top right): *Sculpture flottante, Otterlo*, Marta Pan, Kröller-Müller Museum, Otterlo, Netherlands
71 (bottom): *Two vertical, three horizontal lines*, George Rickey, Kröller-Müller Museum, Otterlo, Netherlands
73 (top left) living façade, European map, Johanna Rossbach, et al., Copenhagen
73 (top right): Maersk head office, Copenhagen, Denmark
73 (middle, bottom): Royal Danish Playhouse, Lundgaard & Tranberg, Copenhagen, Denmark
74 (top): Langebro bridge tower, Kaj Gottlob, Copenhagen, Denmark
74 (bottom left): Royal Danish Library, Schmidt Hammer Lassen, Copenhagen, Denmark
74 (bottom right): Aller Media building, PLH Architects, Copenhagen, Denmark
75 (top): Hotel CPH Living, Copenhagen, Denmark
75 (middle): Langebro bridge, Kaj Gottlob (foreground); Copenhagen Opera House, Henning Larsen (background), Copenhagen, Denmark
75 (upper bottom left): Harbor Bath, PLOT, Copenhagen, Denmark
75 (bottom left): Woodland crematorium, Gunnar Asplund, Stockholm, Sweden
75 (bottom right): *Coral* pendant lightolier, David Trubridge; Hotel Skeppsholmen, Stockholm, Sweden
76 (top): The Woodland Cemetery, Erik Gunnar Asplund/Sigurd Lewerentz, Stockholm, Sweden
76 (middle, bottom), 77: Woodland Chapel, Erik Gunnar Asplund, Stockholm, Sweden
78 (top): Solberga Gård youth hostel, Öland, Sweden
78 (bottom): barn, designer unknown, Sweden
79 (top): Tivoli, Copehagen, Denmark
79 (bottom): cruise ship, harbor, Copehagen, Denmark

80 (top): Frederikskirken, Copenhagen, Denmark
80 (middle left): warehouse building, Nyhavn, Copenhagen, Denmark
80 (middle right): Royal Danish Library, Schmidt Hammer Lassen, Copenhagen, Denmark
80 (bottom left): Børsgade, Copenhagen, Denmark
80 (bottom right): Storkspringvandet, Copenhagen, Denmark
81 (top left): SAS Royal Hotel, Arne Jacobsen, Copenhagen, Denmark
81 (top, middle right): color, Copenhagen, Denmark
81 (middle left): Saint Nikolaj Church, Copenhagen, Denmark
81 (bottom left): railway station, Paul Armin Due, Finse, Norway
81 (bottom right): Flåm railway, Norway
82 (top, middle): Flåm, Norway
82 (bottom): Aurlandsfjord, Norway
83 (top): Nærøyfjord, Norway
83 (middle): Nobel Peace Center, David Adjaye, Oslo, Norway
83 (bottom): Oslo City Hall, Arnstein Arneberg and Magnus Poulsson, Oslo, Norway
84 (top): Viking Ship Museum, Oslo, Norway
84 (bottom): Gol Stave Church, Norwegian Museum of Cultural History, Oslo, Norway
85 (top left): Log House, Norwegian Museum of Cultural History, Oslo, Norway
85 (top right): Norwegian Museum of Cultural History, Oslo, Norway
85 (middle): Oslo City Hall, Arnstein Arneberg and Magnus Poulsson, Oslo, Norway
85 (bottom): National Theater, Henrik Bull, Oslo, Norway
87 (top left) Landschaftspark Duisberg-Nord, Latz & Partner, Duisberg, Germany
87 (top right), 87 (bottom left): Boiler house, Shaft 12, Zeche Zollverein Mine, Fritz Schupp & Martin Kremmer, Essen, Germany
87 (bottom right): escalator, Zeche Zollverein Mine, Rem Koolhaas/ OMA, Essen, Germany
88: Red Dot Design Museum (former boiler house, Shaft 12), adaptive re-use, Norman Foster, Essen, Germany
89: Zollverein School of Management and Design, Kazuyo Sejima & Ryue Nishizawa/ SANAA, Essen, Germany

90: Kolumba Museum, Peter Zumthor, Cologne, Germany
91, 92, 93, 94: Bruder Klaus Chapel, Peter Zumthor, Mechernich, Germany
97, 98, 99, 100: Bregenz Artmuseum, Peter Zumthor, Bregenz, Austria
101 (top): Harbor Building, "The Wave," Nägele, Waibel, Ritsch, Spagolla & Steinmann, Bregenz, Austria
101 (middle, bottom): shop windows, Zurich, Switzerland
102: Heidi Weber Museum, Le Corbusier, Zurich, Switzerland
103: Liner Museum, Gigon/ Guyer Architects, Appenzell, Switzerland
104: Beyeler Foundation, Renzo, Piano, Riehen, Switzerland
105 (top left): Vitra Design Museum, Frank Gehry, Weil am Rhein, Germany
105 (top right, middle): Factory Building, Álvaro Siza, Weil am Rhein, Germany
105 (bottom): Vitra Fire Station, Zaha Hadid, Weil am Rhein, Germany
106 (top): Balancing Tools, Claes Oldenburg & Coosje van Bruggen, Vitra, Weil am Rhein, Germany
106 (middle,bottom), 107, 108: Conference Pavilion, Tadao Ando, Vitra, Weil am Rhein, Germany
109, 110, 111: Vitra Haus, Herzog and deMeuron, Weil am Rhein, Germany
112 (top left): Train station, Basel, Switzerland
112 (top right):YMCA Hostel, Basel
112 (middle right): designer unknown, Basel
112 (middle left, bottom): Sudpark, Herzog and deMeuron, Basel
112 (lower left) Monastère Sainte-Claire, Renzo Piano, Ronchamp, France
113, 114: Chapel of Notre Dame du Haut, Le Corbusier, Ronchamp, France
115, 116 (top): Shelter for Roman ruins, Peter Zumthor, Chur, Switzerland
116 (middle left), sports bar, Chur, Switzerland
116 (middle) Bundner Art Museum, renovations, Peter Zumthor, Chur, Switzerland
116 (middle right) Grand Council Chamber, Rudolph Fontana, Chur, Switzerland
116 (bottom): Zumthor Studio, Peter Zumthor, Haldenstein, Switzerland

117, 118 (top, middle): Thermal Baths, Peter Zumthor, Vals, Switzerland

118 (upper bottom left): village bridge, Jürg Conzett, Vals, Switzerland

118 (bottom): vacation houses, Peter Zumthor, Leis, Switzerland

119 (top): St. James the Greater Chapel, Leis, Switzerland

119 (middle): vacation houses, Peter Zumthor, Leis, Switzerland

119 (bottom left): village bridge, Jürg Conzett, Vals, Switzerland

119 (right): traditional house, Vals, Switzerland

120 Thermal Baths, Peter Zumthor, Vals, Switzerland

121 (top): hotel rooms, Peter Zumthor, Vals, Switzerland

121 (middle left): Vals Gneiss paving, Vals, Switzerland

121 (middle right): Chapel of St. Nikolaus, Vals, Switzerland

121 (bottom): water trough, St. Benedikt Chapel, Peter Zumthor, Sumvitg, Switzerland

122, 123, 124, 125: St. Benedikt Chapel, Peter Zumthor, Sumvitg, Switzerland

126: La Congiunta: Peter Märkli, Giornico, Switzerland

127 (top left): billboard, Ticino, Switzerland

127 (top right): roadside, Ticino, Switzerland

127 (top middle, middle): Mogno, Switzerland

127 (bottom): Chiesa di San Giovanni Battista, Mario Botta, Mogno, Switzerland

129: Convent of Sainte Marie de la Tourette, Le Corbusier, Eveux, France

131 (top): Villa Capra "La Rotunda," Andrea Palladio, Vicenza

131, 132 (top): Brion Cemetery, Carlo Scarpa, San Vito d'Altivole, Italy

132 (middle): Byblos Art Hotel, Alessandro Mendini, Verona, Italy

132 (bottom), 133 (top left): Castelvecchio Museum, Carlo Scarpa, Verona, Italy

133 (top right, middle): Banco Popolare di Verona, Carlo Scarpa, Verona, Italy

133 (upper bottom left), Veneto landscape, Italy

133 (upper bottom right, bottom): Peggy Guggenheim Collection, Venice, Italy

134 (top): Callie, Peggy Guggenheim Collection, Venice, Italy

134 (middle): Doge's Palace, Piazza San Marco, Venice, Italy

134 (bottom left): Piazza San Marco, Venice, Italy
134 (bottom right): street view, Florence, Italy
135 (top): Chiesa di San Croce, Florence, Italy
135 (middle): Duomo, Florence, Italy
135 (bottom left): Relais Columbara, Travo, Italy
135 (bottom right): Peggy & Hugh, Prague, Czech Republic
137 (top left): Old Town Square (Staroměstské náměstí), Prague, Czech Republic
137 (top right): Clock tower, Old Town Square, Prague, Czech Republic
137 (upper left middle): Lesser Town (Mala Strana), Prague, Czech Republic
137 (upper right middle): Vitava River, Prague, Czech Republic
137 (lower left middle), (lower right middle): Lesser Town (Mala Strana), Prague, Czech Republic
137 (bottom): Charles Bridge (Karlův most), Prague, Czech Republic
138 (top left): Nerudova, Prague, Czech Republic
138 (top right, middle): Sax Hotel, Jánský vršek, Prague, Czech Republic
138 (bottom), 139 (top): Jánský vršek, Prague, Czech Republic
139 (bottom): Schwarzenberg Palace, Prague, Czech Republic
140 (top): Jánský vršek, Prague, Czech Republic
140 (middle): Judita Wharf, (Přístav Judita), Prague, Czech Republic
140 (bottom left): Lennon Wall, Prague, Czech Republic
140 (bottom right): St. Salvator Church, (Kostel Nejsvětějšího Salvátora) Prague, Czech Republic
141 (top): Nationale-Nederlanden (Fred & Ginger) building, Frank Gehry & Vladimir Milunic, Prague, Czech Republic
141 (middle upper left, middle right): street scene, Prague, Czech Republic
141 (middle lower left): National Theater New Stage, Karel Prager, Prague, Czech Republic
141 (bottom): view from Petřín Park (Petřínské sady)‚ Prague, Czech Republic
143: Kursaal Congress Center and Auditorium, Rafael Moneo, Donostia-San Sebastian, Spain
144 (top left): Peine del Viento, Eduardo Chilleda, Donostia-San Sebastian, Spain

144 (top right, middle): Chilleda Museum, San Sebastian, Spain
144 (bottom), 145, 146 (top left, middle): Guggenheim Bilbao, Frank Gehry, Bilbao, Spain
146 (top right): Guggenheim Bilbao bridge, Santiago Calatrava, Bilbao, Spain
146 (bottom), 147 (top): Hotel Aire de Bardenas, Emiliano Lopez & Monica Rivera, Tudela, Navarra, Spain
147 (middle left), street view, Palau Güell, Antoni Gaudi, Barcelona, Spain
147 (middle right, bottom), 148, 149: Barcelona Pavilion, Mies van der Rohe, Barcelona, Spain
171: Eskilstuna, Sweden

Author's Biography

Ben Jacks, a designer, architect, writer, and teacher, holds degrees from the University of Chicago, the University of Pennsylvania, and the Stonecoast MFA Program in Creative Writing at the University of Southern Maine. When not looking at buildings and making photographs, he teaches at Miami University, Oxford, Ohio, including courses in beginning design, human behavior, design detailing, and understanding architecture through drawing.

In 1991 Ben walked the Appalachian Trail, 2000 miles from Georgia to his home in Maine. This half-year experience of walking and living outdoors inspired and continues to inform his thinking and writing about architecture, aesthetics, landscape, and place, which has been published in *Journal of Architectural Education, Places*, and *Landscape Journal*.

As a designer, Ben focuses on detail and craft, seeking to develop the potentially rich and intimate relationship between landscape, building, dwelling, and interior. He traces his love of good craft to his maternal grandfather, Hugo Persson, a carpenter, schoolteacher, and labor union organizer, who immigrated to Wisconsin from Eskilstuna, Sweden, much in the manner described in Vilhelm Moberg's *The Emigrants*. Good craft and a job well done perhaps allowed Hugo to feel some control in a new world.

Choosing a hopeful path, and responding to his children's anxiety about the state of our deteriorating environment, Ben is currently at work designing and building a family home meant to last: a flexible-family-structure, aging-in-place, aspiring LEED Platinum, net-zero, Passive House in Cincinnati, Ohio.

We want to remember what these places are like, we are anxious to remember them—they were once part of our youth . . .

–Vilhelm Moberg, *The Emigrants*

CPSIA information can be obtained at www.ICGtesting.com
Printed in the USA
LVIW01n2316240817
546307LV00001B/10